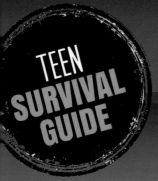

TEEN SURVIVAL GUIDE

SURVIVING BULLIES AND MEAN TEENS

MARY P. DONAHUE, PH.D.

Enslow Publishing
101 W. 23rd Street
Suite 240
New York, NY 10011
USA

enslow.com

Published in 2018 by Enslow Publishing, LLC.
101 W. 23rd Street, Suite 240, New York, NY 10011

Cataloging-in-Publication Data

Names: Donahue, Mary P., Ph.D.
Title: Surviving bullies and mean teens / Mary P. Donahue, Ph.D.
Description: New York : Enslow Publishing, 2018. | Series: Teen survival guide | Includes bibliographical references and index. | Audience: Grades 7-12.
Identifiers: ISBN 9780766091948 (library bound) | ISBN 9780766093683 (pbk.) | ISBN 9780766093690 (6 pack)
Subjects: LCSH: Bullying—Prevention—Juvenile literature. | Bullying—Juvenile literature.
Classification: LCC BF637.B85 D66 2018 | DDC 302.34/3—dc23

Printed in the United States of America

To Our Readers: We have done our best to make sure all websites in this book were active and appropriate when we went to press. However, the author and the publisher have no control over and assume no liability for the material available on those websites or on any websites they may link to. Any comments or suggestions can be sent by email to customerservice@enslow.com.

CONTENTS

INTRODUCTION

There's a curious saying you might have heard before, and it goes kinda like this: I want to be unique, just like everyone else.

You are made up of your own special ingredients—and your teen years are where those things gel into a specialized, awesome version of you. It's also where fitting in becomes most important. You want to express yourself individually, and you want to be valued and accepted into a group. That can be super complicated. You're developing friendships that could last for a day or a lifetime. It's exciting! But there are stumbling blocks, too. One of the most difficult situations is when you run into bullies or when the mean teens get you in their sights. Sometimes bullying happens in public, where people can see. More and more often, however, it happens under the radar—through nasty notes, gossip, rumors, or on social media. Either way, it hurts. A lot.

This book is written to help you navigate the difficult situation that is bullying. It will help you figure out what bullying really is, as opposed to just having a couple of bad days. You'll learn about teen groups who have additional pressures. Those groups include teens caught up in unsafe romantic relationships, kids with intellectual or physical diff-

There's a lot of future left for you. The decisions you make today, including about who you hang out with, matter a lot. Choose wisely!

abilities (which are not dis-abilities, just different ones), and those who identify with sexual or gender diversity.

In certain places in this book, you'll run into a few words you might not be sure of. We're here to help! One word is "non-binary." This refers to people who don't feel like their birth gender. So, a kid might have been designated a boy at birth but not feel quite like a boy. They may not feel quite like a girl, either. 'Non-binary' means that gender, for them, isn't an either/or thing. Another word is 'cisgender.' This is used to refer to people who do identify according to the gender they were assigned when they were born. Using these terms is not a political statement—and we definitely don't want to tell you what to think or feel. It's simply a means of helping you to recognize added vocabulary. The point to keep in mind is that teens who have diff-abilities or are experiencing sexual or gender challenges may have to deal with more serious bullying problems and worse outcomes. And we think you should know that.

We're also going explore some myths about bullying. You'll learn how to decide for yourself what you think. And, of course, since it wouldn't be a book about bullying without talking about the internet, we'll talk cyberbullying—which can really play games with your head! But don't worry, we're going to give you a skill to help your brain catch up to your feelings. Then you'll get good advice and instruction on how to form a safe space with people who can help you stop the bullying. Read this guide slowly, so you can really think about your situation and how to change it for the better. Chances are, it's more complicated but more solvable than it looks. And you have more strength than you think. Just go slow and steady, and you'll be able to move forward.

You got this!

CHAPTER ONE

BULLIES OR BLUSTER

You're a teenager! Which can mean life is super confusing for lots of reasons. The biggest is probably that you're still figuring out who you are—such as what matters to you and who you want to be. Some kids really value being independent, for example, while others enjoy being on a team. Some want to work quietly and others like attention or awards. At school, you're learning how to do you as much as you're learning from your books. You're also probably getting lots of messages about your worth from the outside world—such as TV shows, your parents, or the internet. Sure, adults were your main buddies when you were younger, but now you're more focused on your friends and fitting in. Who you hang out with starts to change who you are!

ARGUING VS. BULLYING

First, let's figure out the difference between regular teen conflict (like having bad day) and actual bullying. Kids argue,

These teens are involved in a mutual dispute. "Mutual" means that they each have a chance to get their point across. Though unpleasant, it doesn't rise to the level of "bullying."

who doesn't? Disagreements can be useful. They can teach you about fairness and negotiation. Sometimes your fight can be a misunderstanding that is easily cleared up, and sometimes someone is being stubborn and insisting on being right. But you and your friend (or friends) want to work out the problem or maybe even agree to disagree and move on. It's can be unpleasant, but it's workable. When it's been more than a few days, however, and your belly starts to hurt, it's time to take a closer look.

A common definition of bullying is that it happens between two people with different influence. So maybe you're being hassled by a more popular student, a teacher who controls your grade, or even a boyfriend you really like! And these disagreements don't happen only a few times. Bullies hurt by repeatedly teasing, gossiping, or otherwise attacking you. It's a form of social power; they act badly in order to make you feel less than them so they can gain (or keep) their status above you.

If you think about it, the need to be in the in crowd surrounds you. We are living in a time when popularity is power. It feels like everyone is fighting to be cool, from Hollywood to Washington, DC. People want to be unique enough to be respected and to fit in enough to be accepted. It's complicated! You've probably noticed that you are your fellow teens are divided into different groups, and you're always working to get in, stay in, or move up! Being different doesn't always play well. Maybe someone is too smart, too quiet, has a disability, dates the wrong person, or dresses in an unusual way. Being different can mean being a target. Enter bullying as a strategy to rule.

If only we could recognize cruel people by how they look! This guy hides his eyes and looks secretive. It would be easy to label him dangerous . . .

WHAT MAKES A BULLY?

You might have an idea about what a bully looks like—
someone with hidden eyes and bad grades, who is really
tough, talks back, and is maybe a loner. The truth is, bullies
can often look like everyone else. Bullies can even be people
you've grown up with and thought were your friends. At
some point, the other kid starts to need influence of some
kind. But how can he or she get it? Bullies know what other

... and how could this sweet girl possibly be mean? Remember, it's not how someone looks that tells you who they are, it's what they do — especially when no one's looking.

people expect and have figured out which kids, teachers, and others they need to act nice to in order to get attention or help. But bullies also know which kids they can take advantage of.

Instead of celebrating variety, bullies use differences to put down someone they see as lesser than themselves. Strategy-wise, here's another difference in gender:

- **Boys** are usually aggressive and bully 'out loud' in front of others. They often prefer to do things like yell insults, trip kids, or play keep-away.

- **Girls** are sometimes more secretive about it; they like to use things like gossip, rumors, social snubbing, and sneering.
- **Non-binary** kids can also bully through shame or by taking advantage of social ignorance.
- And cyber-bullying seems to be **open to all!**

WHY BULLIES HURT

Wonder why a bully lashes out? Many bullies prefer to work under the radar, sometimes even with a smile. They can be sweet and nice and then turn nasty at just the right

FRIENDS WITHOUT FEAR

Remember that bully abuse is a pattern of behavior. It's not just one time. It makes you feel awful, and it keeps coming. In a healthy relationship, you want to give and get respect. You want to trust each other to take care of the friendship, even when you aren't together in the same place. You should be able to have friends without fear. Sometimes you disagree, but you work it out together. You don't hold it against each other later. In a balanced relationship, you're supposed to lift each other up, give courage to try things, share ideas, and be considerate of other opinions.

time. If you know the reason behind their cruelty, it could help you. Here are some possible explanations:

- They're bored and need to create some drama or deflect from themselves.
- They thrive on being 'important' and gain status by feeding off a more vulnerable person.
- They were the target before and want to get even somehow.
- They're mad at the world.

Whatever the reason, they chose someone like you because they think they can rule you. You might be someone who isn't really noticeable, who worries about belonging, or who can be sad, shy, anxious, or quiet. Maybe you think the treatment you receive is normal or acceptable, or you know it's wrong but don't know how to make things different. You probably don't like to be the center of attention, either. One thing we do know is that when you're being bullied, you usually think things are your fault. You look for ways to change yourself, hoping it will stop. Bullies choose people who they're pretty sure won't come up against them, or who at least won't win if they do.

Popular kids can be very effective bullies. They take advantage of being seen as good leaders or as cool kids. Acting secretly horrible gives them status; they're fed by the support of their followers. Bullies are out to satisfy their own needs. Though it hurts you a lot and sometimes permanently—to the bully, it's nothing personal.

But when you keep getting treated badly, you begin to act differently. Maybe you skip school a lot, quit activities, get more angry or snappy, worry a lot, eat and sleep less or more, and your grades might drop. Without a doubt, it's a pretty terrible time. And because you're afraid, don't want to make things worse, or don't like attention, you don't tell. It can seem hopeless. Those feelings are real, even if the reality is different. Fortunately, things can change.

CHAPTER TWO

JUST ADD PRESSURE

Everyone wants to fit in and feel normal. Of course, the question is, "What's normal?" Here's a secret: it doesn't exist. Normal means something different to everyone. It changes as we change. But the bummer is that even though we're all human, not everyone is treated equally. Kids with physical differences, gaps in social skills, prejudice, and different health needs are generally bullied more and helped less. For these teens, the environment needs major upgrades! Let's consider some groups that might be struggling.

DEVELOPMENTALLY DELAYED AND INTELLECTUAL OR PHYSICAL DIFFERENCES

You've read about brain development. If you've been to health class, you know there are lots of ways kids can develop outside of what people consider normal. What if you have some diff-

Use this scale to decide how others make you feel. Is that level okay with you? Does something need to change?

-ability that's picked up by mean people? Chances are pretty good that it will be used against you—even more than if you were a typically-abled kid. It's true. Studies done by the US Health and Human Services show that special education (SpEd) kids are at a higher risk for physical, mental, and cyberbullying, and they experience higher levels of mental distress compared to non-SpEd kids. In fact, even teachers and school staff can be less kind to SpEd students. Yes, even people who have been trained and should know better sometimes become harmers rather than helpers. We hope that schools won't do this on purpose, of course. In terms of results, however, it doesn't matter. Already super-challenged kids are in an even tighter spot; regardless of intent, big hurt happens.

LESBIAN, GAY, BISEXUAL, TRANSSEXUAL, QUESTIONING, AND MORE (LGBTQ+) TEENS

S-E-X, SeX, SEX! There are so many messages about sex and sexuality that the real deal—your personal identity—gets lost.

Sexuality and gender sometimes makes people nervous. There are lots of mixed messages about what's right and how things should be. Those messages can make you feel isolated, ashamed, or afraid. Now multiply that by about a billion for LGBTQ+ kids. For sure, the teen world is pretty tough on kids who are exploring alternatives. Think about it: from birth, your private parts have decided how you act, what you play with, how you dress—either boy or girl. Yup! You get judged first by your body parts, not who you can be.

As an LGBTQ+ teen, you also have fewer places to go for information. Maybe you don't even know the questions to ask! You might be afraid that someone will catch on and out

These kids are rocking their support! Parades and demonstrations are important ways to let yourself and your friends know that they are not alone. Private support is important, too!

you before you're ready or are even really sure about things. Homophobia is widespread in teen society, with limited professional research on it or support for change. Not only that, you often end up teaching others about stuff you're only just finding out yourself. It's emotionally and mentally exhausting!

The Health and Human Services research tells us that 1 in 3 kids today identifies as cisgender gay or non-binary.

It's hard to know for sure, however, because lots of you probably don't feel safe enough to tell. That's because LGBTQ+ kids tend to experience twice as much physical violence as other teens; negative messages delivered directly or disguised as innocent jokes, which are acted out in stereotypical gags or via pranks; a higher risk for suicidal thoughts, attempts, and completions; and higher incidents of substance abuse, rape, high risk behavior, and homelessness.

Growing up is already complicated enough. You're struggling to figure out who you're going to be. If you're an LGBTQ+ kid, you're even less supported by peers, schools, and communities. Where do you turn? It isn't surprising if you're pretty angry. It's understandable.

THEY LOOK LIKE TIGERS

When dealing with a bully, there's a very useful quote to keep in mind from author Alice Walker: "Nobody is as powerful as we make them out to be." This means that chances are pretty high you have more of your own power than you think. Use some of that power to reach out. Once you decide the problem can use some outside help, breathe deep and sit for a minute. Congratulate yourself for taking the first step in creating a safe space.

BULLIES IN ROMANCE

Dating is a big part of teen life. It's important to feel accepted and valued by someone you love. Dreamy relationships are nice for sure. But some can quickly turn into unequal, controlling bonds that are dangerous. Your partner begins to control you in ways that seem innocent enough at first. Like he or she wants to spend every spare minute with you and only you. It feels nice, right? Eventually, however, you're not allowed to talk to some people or your partner will get mad. And you're only allowed to wear certain clothing. Soon, you're changing your hair, avoiding friends, giving up clubs, having to be available by phone at all times, and giving over your passwords. No matter how hard you try, though, it seems as if you're always doing something wrong. There's name-calling and careless comments that don't really seem bad, but actually make you feel terrible. There could even be a slap, a pinch, or a shove. Instead of being happy, you're feeling afraid, ashamed, or embarrassed. And you're always making excuses. You cut yourself off from other people, trying to be everything your partner needs you to be. Maybe they force you to do things you don't want to do, like steal stuff, use alcohol, or send sexy pictures. You often feel uncomfortable, afraid, or humiliated.

Repeated bullying in romance is also called dating abuse. And it is way too common. In fact, studies by the

These two people are having a rough moment, for sure — it happens!
But it is important to feel heard and valued in your relationship.

National Coalition Against Domestic Violence report that
almost 1 in 4 girls and 1 in 7 boys experience some form of
teen dating abuse. Take a look at the kids around you; it's
possible someone in your group will be hurt by his or her
dating partner. And because it often happens in secret, he
or she might not know how to get out. Way less than half of
teenagers ever tell anyone about it. Some don't even know
it's wrong. Without help, it can follow you into adulthood
and poison your life.

CLOUDY WITH A CHANCE OF CLARITY: BULLYING MYTHS

Up until now, you've been taught stuff. You've taken tests to see if you've learned it. And you'll use a lot of that learning from now on. You've also heard and learned things from friends and maybe online that seem true, so you believe it.

Now your brain is bigger and more is coming at you every day. You're questioning things. How do you know if what people tell you is what you really believe? You have to collect your own information. If something doesn't feel right, it might not be. Because your life will grow really fast from here on out, why not do your own thinking and help your brain to grow with you?

So, here's a chance to practice your thinking. Below are a number of popular myths for you to think about, and what the research really says about these popular misconceptions.

Take some time to pay attention to what's going on around you. Really examine what you see and hear. Then make your opinion. Critical thinking is an important skill.

Myth: The target is weak

Reality: Hurting people is about the bully's needs and immediate rewards; it is definitely not about you. Power is so often mental: a physically strong boy can be bullied by a small girl; a differently-abled kid can taunt jocks; and even strangers can ridicule and intimidate very effectively! Size and strength do NOT matter. And bullies think ahead. They set things up for their own advantage. If you want to fight back with fists or words, the bully often still has the upper hand.

Myth: Being bullied helps build character

Reality: Instead of building character, continual bullying causes emotional injury and illness that can last a lifetime. It can even change how your body works, according to the work done by UNH and Dr. Malcolm Davis. Bullying victims can suffer depression, anxiety, fear, confusion, and more. This is serious stuff!

Myth: Bullies are scared, hurt kids inside

Reality: While this thinking used to be accepted, much more research has been done in the past few decades. Guess what? It turns out that bullies generally have higher self-esteem than their peers. Not only that, but they're often among the cool kids. They have social power, they need to keep their popularity, and they like to be in charge. They have followers—other kids want to impress them. They have huge influence and use it to intimidate. Nope, as the good researchers at UNH found, "bullies are kids with problems, but low self-esteem is usually not one of them."

Myth: If you're neither the target nor the bully, you shouldn't get involved

Reality: Bystanders are very important allies in stopping the problem. The bully, remember, is looking for power—

laughter, admiration, tears, or fear—and if you're silently standing by, you're contributing to that power. Not only that, but you could get hurt by your own inaction. Did you know that just by watching someone get bullied and hurt, you could become depressed or afraid, have trouble trusting others, feel less safe yourself, and experience guilt or shame?

Bullying is toxic. The general rule is if you see it, say it.

Myth: Jealousy and possessiveness are a sign of true love.

Reality: These are actually signs that the person sees you as a possession. It's a common early warning sign of abuse. In a controlling dating relationship, your partner believes they are entitled to restrict your rights; they use words, fists, friends, sex, money, transportation, and a whole lot of other things to maintain their power. What it boils down to is that they see you as less than equal. That's nothing to do with love.

Myth: Kids will grow out of it.

Reality: They often don't. Who'd want to? If bullies are rewarded by social status, minions, lunch money, and attention—and aren't held accountable—who'd want to stop doing it? Indeed, bad behavior can actually bond group members together! (NOTE: Respectful behavior also bonds people together, too! Just sayin'.)

Parents need to put work and devices aside and give their full attention to their child's scary—and risky!—request for help.

Myth: Asking for help from adults will only make it worse.

Reality: You should never have to deal with bullying and mean teens alone, though you might try to at first. Part of the bullying might include statements such as, "What, you gonna tell your mommy?" This feels awful! Statements like

ADULT FYI

Message for adults: You should be careful about how you help a child who is being bullied. Acting hastily can, at the very least, cause you to miss an opportunity to correct, teach, and inspire. Since the bad behavior is fueled by emotion (rather than informed by logic), you must be careful and go slow. Believe the teen, listen to what he or she has to say, observe his or her actions. And read Chapter 5.

There are a lot more myths out there. Using your developing critical thinking skills, you can work to see the truth!

that are meant to challenge you and keep you silent. Don't fall for it! If you've tried to talk sense to the group or avoid the meanness in other ways and it hasn't worked, it's time to rally the troops!

CHAPTER FOUR

ONLINE AND OUT OF LINE

The internet is great for keeping up with friends, parties, and more! You can text or email something you just thought of or make plans with lots of different people all at once. There's a lot of school stuff that happens online, too, and when you're on the internet, you're never out of the loop.

Unfortunately, bullies and mean teens can use the internet to hurt and manipulate. This is called cyberbullying; it happens when people use computers, cell phones, and more to access texts, emails, pictures, and social media sites to harass or embarrass you. Just like with in-person bullying, with cyberbulling there's a power difference between the bully and you, and it happens repeatedly. Here are some ways cyberbullying can happen:

- Someone teases and says scary or mean things to you online.
- A rumor starts and gets picked up by several people at once, and then spreads like wildfire.

When you're on the internet, use important safegaurds like working near your parents. That way they can check on you—and you can quickly ask for help if you need it.

- Your passwords get out and someone logs on as you, then they say mean, awful stuff about others under your name.
- Pictures or videos are taken of you in private places, such as the gym or a dressing area, and are posted online.

29

- Someone who is no longer a friend can post past private conversations or pictures for everyone to see.

ONLINE VERSUS IN-PERSON

This awesome research team from the University of New Hampshire, which has been studying bullying for a long time, finds that 1 in 3 kids online has been cyberbullied. That's a lot! It's important to know how cyberbullying is different from the in-person harassment because it makes a difference in how it's fixed. Here's what you need to know:

- Cyberbullying can happen 24/7, the bully doesn't have to be anywhere near you, and you might not know at first that it's happening.
- Cyberbullying can spread very fast and really far.
- Cyberbullying is harder to get away from because so much of your life happens online.
- The material from cyberbullying lasts forever.
- Cyberbullying often happens anonymously.

That last one—that cyberbullying can be anonymous—is the kicker. As teens, you know how you should behave in public, but you act the way you want to in private. (Think about it. You're less likely to swear in front of your grandmother than your best friend, right?) So, when there's no face-to-face interaction involved, people can say things they would never say in person. It's also harder to prove, because bullies often have accounts under different names. So what do you do?

OH, BEHAVE!

First, you need to remember that the internet isn't as private as people think. Once you post things, you lose control of what happens to them. Anyone who sees your stuff can screen shot or cut-and-paste it. So the most important thing you can do to help yourself avoid online bullying is to set your privacy settings so that only trusted people can see

The internet can be a scary place; it can make you feel terrible and alone. If you're feeling scared, ask for help right away!

31

your posts and information. And don't friend people you don't know; they could be anyone, including someone who wants to troll your account. Then, be aware of what you're putting out there yourself. If you're going to rant about a teacher or even send a private message about one friend to another friend, it's possible the person you're talking bad about will see it somehow. And finally, keep your passwords to yourself. Even a friend you trust could end up giving them away. It happens a lot.

ASAP SOS

Everyone gets curious. Sometimes, you might see something online that you click on, even though you know your shouldn't. You might even start having a conversation with a stranger that is fun at first, but it can turn nasty. You might start to feel scared or embarrassed. But you don't know what to do because you weren't supposed to be doing this in the first place. Honestly, you need to involve an adult. Right away. They can keep you safe. Maybe you'll get a lecture, but that's a small price compared to the trouble that comes from cyberbullying. The lecture will end; cyber-trouble doesn't.

YOU'RE BEING CYBERBULLIED!

It's okay. There are still things you can do.

- **Do not answer the bully back**. This is the best thing you can do. If you do, two things will happen. First, they know that you have seen their nonsense and it will spur them on. Second, you have given them more words to use against you.
- **Block the person.** You might feel the need to read everyone's comments, but there's no sense in it. It'll only hurt more and give the bully more space in your head. You might even lose it and do or say something that makes you look like the jerk!
- **Report the cyberbullying.** Most social media sites have places to do that. Schools, too, are getting more involved in cyberbullying because of how much schooling is done on computers. And don't forget the police. Especially if threats, private pictures, sexting, or hate speech is part of the situation, the police can help. They've got high-tech ways to trace sites. And, trust us. Your adults need to know this is happening.

Above all, learn the breathing exercise from the next chapter. It's super important for you to approach this complicated experience with as much clarity and logic as possible. Then you can make your plans. Up until now, the bully has had the upper hand. Let's see how you might change that.

WHAT DO TURTLES HAVE TO DO WITH THIS?

Move slowly and steadily. Remember the kid's book about the turtle and the rabbit? "Slow and steady wins the race." It's true. Bullying creates chaos; it's meant to keep you hopping. We're going to slow things down to help you work it out and move forward.

Break Time!

Let's slow down and practice how to breathe. Really. Learn this coping skill and it'll help change your life. Seriously! Focus on sensing and listening to your breath. Here's how: Stick your belly out. Now breathe deep for four seconds, taking breath right down to the bottom of your lungs. Hold it for four seconds. And exhale slowly but deeply, so your belly presses in against your spine. Wait again for four seconds. (Sometimes it helps to put your hand on your stomach when doing all this; it keeps the focus on your midsection.) Do it again. You should notice you feel a

Taking a short break can help clear your mind. You'll be amazed by how much you can get done once you've taken a moment to breathe.

little calmer. If you do this four times, then you've learned deep breathing. Some call it "4 Square Breathing" because they imagine each side of a square as they're doing the steps. Either way, when practiced often, it can become second nature to you; it should kick in without you even noticing. These forty-eight seconds can help in all kinds of anxiety-provoking situations—hopefully for the rest of your life! But you gotta practice. It will make things more clear because it allows the thinking parts of the brain to catch up.

All right, have you given your body a minute to rest so your brain catches up? Slowly and steadily. Are you there? Cool. Next, decide on some safe adults to employ in your cause. It's critical here that you feel heard and understood, and that starts with knowing what you want to say. It's a good idea to write out bullet points to help organize your thoughts. Recognize that what you're going through hurts and try to keep the emotion off to the side for now.

SHAPING THE SQUAD!

Bullying is very hard to stop by yourself. You're going to need to ask some people to help you figure out what to do and how to best do it. This will be your squad. Most often a parent or guardian is the first choice because they have legal responsibility for you. You could then add a trusted teacher, coach, or relative. You want people who can look at things from different viewpoints. They add a layer of perspective. Keep your squad small but talented. Before you approach squad members, however, help yourself out and do the following:

- Write down your main points—who's doing what, the methods used, witnesses, times, dates, etc.
- Be detailed with facts.
- Take screenshots, videos, or voice recordings.

- Write out what you've tried to do about it, such as who you might have already talked to, and what did or didn't happen.
- Develop ideas for resolution; it's useful to present problems with potential solutions.

These actions will show the pattern of behavior. It also helps you get your thoughts straight, away from the emotion. Now, here's how to approach adult helpers:

- Go slowly when you finally talk to them and maintain eye contact. This is serious business, and you want to communicate that.
- Be direct; don't hint. Say things like, "I need help. Really."
- Use your lists.
- If you tell your story and it falls flat, reorganize your thoughts and try again. Perhaps your adult won't know what you're trying to say at first. Be aware that they might be distracted with worry about you or at least not expecting this serious subject.
- Present your concerns at a calm time, not just before practice or crazy dinnertime. Consider making an appointment just for this talk. Ask your aunt to lunch, text dad about a good time for a sit down, email your teacher for an appropriate private conversation time.

After you've had these talks with your supportive adults, you've formed your squad! Now, all you need to do is get organized as a team.

BANDING THE BUNCH!

So, you're all sitting together and have decided, as a team, that something needs to be done about your situation. You have collected some evidence. Now you have to figure out how to go about making a plan. Consider the following:

- Someone needs to take the lead. Most often it's your parent. They'll need good input from you so they know exactly what's going on and how to move forward.

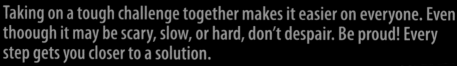

Taking on a tough challenge together makes it easier on everyone. Even thhough it may be scary, slow, or hard, don't despair. Be proud! Every step gets you closer to a solution.

- Some teams write out the squad goals for this getting-better campaign. It helps to keep everyone focused. This is an emotionally difficult situation, so written points keep the goal central.
- You all might need some guidelines for communication, too, given how crazy life can get. The squad should decide about how best to relay information, i.e., by group email, phone, or over coffee.
- Texting intense or long blocks of information is not recommended because of the potential for others to misread or respond too quickly. Emails can be read and answered at a slower pace, which aids fact digestion.
- You might be frustrated or afraid, but keeping your wits about you is key. Take time for respectful communication. Know who you're talking to. You wouldn't talk to the principal the same way you talk to your friends. Talk to people in the same way that you'd want to be spoken to in that situation.
- Many school districts now have anti-bully programs. But some don't use those standards without being reminded. As your squad gets to work, be sure someone gets the job of finding out about school district rules, as well as federal, state, and local laws. If you have to play hardball, knowing all that info will help!

TO CALL THE BULLY'S PARENTS—OR NOT

Sometimes, teams want to confront the bully's parents or guardian. This may not be the best thing. Careful consideration is suggested about whether or not to directly contact the bully's people. Here's why:

- Your personal privacy is very important. Imagine accidentally giving away private information such as your identity, your diff-ability, or even your sexual identity before you're ready. Advantage: not you.

- The place where the bullying is happening might have more information than you do about past incidents, probations, etc. To protect both you and other kids, it's often better for the team to involve outside help, like a principal, the police, a coach, or some other manager. They might have useful special knowledge or some administrative influence.

- Make copies of what you give to anyone. Keep records of interactions, such as who you spoke to, when, why, and the results. Know what you hope will happen. FYI: It's better to frame your goal as the need for the bullying to stop versus wanting punishment or revenge. Bitterness never helps. At the same time, however, bullies need consequences that are meaningful to them. So, figure out how to keep those two things balanced in your mind.

- The team needs to help each other stay on message; refrain from gossip, passing rumors, and dissing bullies, bystanders, or other adults. That tends to spoil your efforts and spend energy needlessly.
- Read that last one again. It's very important. Don't become what you're trying to stop.

The adults who are helping you will need know that while the team is gathering information and planning, you're still being exposed to the bullying, you're still confused, and you can't be expected to be organized and rational at all times. They need to be the voice of reason. You guys need to discuss what you want and why. For example, you may not want to involve the school administration; other team members may feel differently. You're in this together, so as a team you have to figure out how to listen to each other's concerns and make the best decision— which isn't always the preferred one.

YOU, AND ONLY YOU

Finally, here's the part that people tend to dismiss, and it's important: self-care. It makes a huge difference to how the getting-better campaign works. Honestly, if you're not taking care of yourself, why expect that others will? Makes sense, right?

So here's what you do:

(1) As the target, it's super important to protect yourself

from further harm. For example, block phone numbers and social media handles of jerky people. Consider going off social media for a while. Sleep without electronics in your room. It'll help you relax. If necessary, ask your family for help.

(2) Your brain can't think without nourishment. Keep hydrated and eat something each day. Take vitamin-type drinks if you can't swallow food. Keep up good hygiene.

Stretch your legs — and exercise your mind! Any time your body is working, it's also helping your brain.

(3) Refrain from using unprescribed substances; besides being illegal (the discovery of which will ruin your case), they don't help in the long term. Things just get worse, and over time, you lose.

(4) Exercise. Even walking releases endorphins, which are natural stress relievers.

(5) Keep your fight private from friends who don't need to know; it allows your plans to have more power. It stops gossip, too.

(6) Change all your passwords and NEVER give them to people (other than your caregivers) again. It's unbelievable how much power you're handing over when you do that. Everything from these accounts has your name, and things last forever.

(7) Admit things that need admitting. If you've sent embarrassing pictures, or if you're talking with strangers online, your safe adults needs to know. If they get sidelined while advocating for you, they could look pretty foolish. And much trust is lost.

(8) Keep communicating with your team. Don't shut people out or stop doing activities if you can possibly help it. Isolation makes the symptoms worse!

(9) Seek information regarding specialty groups, if possible. Dating abuse, suicide, sexual assault, transgender, and a whole host of other specialties have local or national hotlines that you can call. Safe adults can also use these hotlines as a means of learning more to help you.

(10) Consider seeking qualified mental health therapy from someone who is familiar with bullying and other forms of abuse. Here's where supportive emotional work can happen. Processing with the help of an unbiased, unconditional professional can help set you up for a pleasant, productive future.

Remember to move—with your team—calmly and steadily. Going forward slowly is still going forward.
Good luck on your journey!

GLOSSARY

aggressive Appearing ready to attack, being forceful.

anonymous Made or written by someone unknown or unnamed.

bystander A person standing nearby but not participating in whatever is happening.

endorphins Chemicals in your body, especially your brain, that scientists believe can help you to feel good and relieve pain.

harass To bother a great deal or to make a very unpleasant situation by uninvited attention.

LGBTQ Lesbian, Gay, Bisexual, Transgender, and Queer. The Q can also mean "questioning one's sexual identity."

myth A popular belief that is actually untrue.

navigate To control one's course or direction.

perspective The ability to see how things really relate to one another.

self-care Taking personal care of yourself, usually involves eating well, sleeping, and exercise, among other activities for the good of your well-being.

sexting Sexually explicit messages (text or image) sent via cell phone.

stereotype An idea that people may have about someone or something that's false or only partially true.

FURTHER READING

BOOKS

Lohmann, M.S., L.P.C., Raychelle Cassada, and Julia V. Taylor, Ph.D. *The Bullying Workbook for Teens: Activities to Help You Deal with Social Aggression and Cyberbullying.* Danvers, MA: Harmony Publishing, 2013

Mayrock, Aija. The Survival Guide to Bullying: Written by a Teen. New York, NY: Scholastic Inc., 2015

Wilson, Reid and Lynn Lyons, LICSW. *Anxious Kids, Anxious Parents: 7 Ways to Stop the Worry Cycle and Raise Courageous & Independent Children.* Deerfield Beach, FL: Health Communications, Inc., 2013

Wiseman, Rosalind. *Queen Bees and Wannabes, 3rd Edition: Helping Your Daughter Survive Cliques, Gossip, Boys, and the New Realities of Girl World.* Danvers, MA: Harmony Books, 2016

WEBSITES

StopBullyingNow US Department of Health and Human Services

https://www.stopbullying.gov

This website offers a diverse education on bullying and staying safe in school. It offers reports, brochures, handouts, images, and webisodes regarding bullying in all sorts of situations typically encountered by kids and teens.

Understanding Bullying

https://extension.unh.edu

Developed by renowned researcher, author, and trainer Dr. Malcolm Smith and his squad, this guide is a great way to help parents and children to understand why/how bullying happens. It offers solutions for the victim, bystanders, and bullies themselves. Check out the checklists!

INDEX